WH

SELECTED POEMS

ESSENTIAL TRANSLATIONS SERIES 12

 Canada Council Conseil des Arts
for the Arts du Canada

 ONTARIO ARTS COUNCIL
CONSEIL DES ARTS DE L'ONTARIO
50 YEARS OF ONTARIO GOVERNMENT SUPPORT OF THE ARTS
50 ANS DE SOUTIEN DU GOUVERNEMENT DE L'ONTARIO AUX ARTS

Guernica Editions Inc. acknowledges the support of the Canada Council
for the Arts and the Ontario Arts Council.
The Ontario Arts Council is an agency of the Government of Ontario.
We acknowledge the financial support of the Government of Canada through
the Canada Book Fund (CBF) for our publishing activities.

FRANCIS CATALANO

WHERE SPACES GLOW

SELECTED POEMS

Translated from the French by Christine Tipper

French-English Bilingual Edition

GUERNICA
TORONTO · BUFFALO · BERKELEY (CA) · LANCASTER (U.K.)
2013

Copyright © 1999, Francis Catalano and Écrits des Forges
Original title: *Romamor*
Copyright © 2001, Francis Catalano and Éditions Trait d'Union
Original title: *Index*
Copyright © 2010, Francis Catalano and Éditions de l'Hexagone
Original title: *Qu'une lueur des lieux*
Copyright © 2013, Christine Tipper and Guernica Editions Inc.
Interview: Copyright © 2013, Christine Tipper and Guernica Editions Inc.
Interview: Copyright © 2013, Antonio D'Alfonso and Francis Catalano.
The interview between Antonio D'Alfonso and Francis Catalano was first
published in *Panoram Italia Montreal*, Vol. 8 No. 2 (April-May 2013).
All rights reserved. The use of any part of this publication,
reproduced, transmitted in any form or by any means, electronic,
mechanical, photocopying, recording or otherwise stored in a
retrieval system, without the prior consent of the publisher is an
infringement of the copyright law. All rights reserved. The use of any part of
this publication, reproduced, transmitted in any form or by any means,
electronic, mechanical, photocopying, recording or otherwise stored in a
retrieval system, without the prior consent of the publisher
is an infringement of the copyright law.

Michael Mirolla, Editor
Guernica Editions Inc.
P.O. Box 117, Station P, Toronto (ON), Canada M5S 2S6
2250 Military Road, Tonawanda, N.Y. 14150-6000 U.S.A.

Typesetting by Antonio D'Alfonso
Distributors:
University of Toronto Press Distribution,
5201 Dufferin Street, Toronto, (ON), Canada M3H 5T8
Small Press Distribution, 1341 Seventh St., Berkeley, CA 94710-1409 U.S.A.
Gazelle Book Services, White Cross Mills, High Town, Lancaster LA1 4XS U.K.
First edition.
Printed in Canada.
Typesetting by Antonio D'Alfonso
Legal Deposit – Fourth Quarter
Library of Congress Catalog Card Number: 2013931298
Library and Archives Canada Cataloguing in Publication
Catalano, Francis, 1961-
[Poems. Selections]
Where spaces glow: selected poems / Francis Catalano; translated
by Christine Tipper.
(Essential translations series; 12)
Also issued in electronic format.
Poems in French with English translations.
ISBN 978-1-55071-699-3
I. Tipper, Christine II. Title. III. Series: Essential translations
series; 12

PS8555.A795A6 2013	C841'.54	C2013-900640-0

CONTENTS

INDEX

Amérique terre archaïque 12
America archaic earth 13
Ici j'assiste dans toute sa grâce 14
Here I assist in all its glory 15
Laurentia tapie sous l'Amérique 16
Laurentia crouched under America 17
Accroupi au bord de l'abîme je m'imagine 18
Crouched by the side of the abyss I imagine 19
L'ombre d'un cervidé m'appâte 20
The shadow of a deer lures me in 21
Il neigeait doucement 22
It was gently snowing 23
Des visages ravinés sombrent çà et là 24
Furrowed faces slump here and there 25
Le pôle vie le pôle mort entre les deux dériver 26
The pole alive the pole dead between the two drifting 27
Tenace race de Siam perdure 28
Tenacious race of Siam endures 29
Marcher et inventer font un 30
Walking and inventing are one and the same 31

ROMAMOR

Splendeur des yeux dessillés 36
Splendour of eyes unsealed 37
En filigrane du rêve, qui va là? 38
In the haziness of a dream, who goes there? 39
Depuis le rectangle de la chambrette 40
From the rectangle of the small bedroom 41
Derrière les murs il est des murs 42
Behind the walls are walls 43

Vus d'en bas les toits de tuiles 44
Seen from below the curved tiled roofs 45
Lire un livre tel l'aruspice 46
Read a book like an aruspice 47
Un touriste avance, avance 48
A tourist advances, advances 49
D'ici part tout le pavé romain 50
From here all the Roman cobblestones leave 51
À l'arrêt j'attends, muet 52
At the bus stop I wait, mute 53
Adolescent, mes rêves les plus chers 54
Adolescent, my dearest dreams 55
Après un mois d'averses 56
After a month of showers 57
Le front plaqué au ciel je traverse 58
My forehead stuck against the sky I cross 59
Les églises sont les tendons mystiques 60
Churches are the mystical tendons 61
Sur l'échiquier, pré géométrique 62
On the chessboard, geometric field 63
Écrire un livre sur rien, absolument 64
Write a book about nothing, absolutely 65
Clore les yeux à double tour 66
Lock your eyes tight 67
Au tintement des cloches 68
With the pealing of the bells 69
Les idées, concepts ou images 70
Ideas, concepts or images 71
Brunissent le soir les pastels de la ville 72
Tingeing brown the town's evening pastels 73

WHERE SPACES GLOW

Le ciel en petites coupures à plates 78
The Sky in Little Slices with Flat 79
Ariz Arias Ariens Arizona 80
Ariz Arias Ariens Arizona 81
Le blanc vin l'herbe 82

The White Wine the Grass 83
Si le soleil est l'oeuf la terre (je m'en veux) 84
If the Sun Is the Egg the Earth (I Blame Myself) 85
L'Apache Trail la paix 86
The Apache Trail Peace 87
L'œuf le bœuf la bouffe 88
The Bull's-Eye the Bull the Bill 89
The West ouais oui ouest 90
The West Yeah Yes Ouest 91
Du Painted Desert j'ai ram- 92
From The Painted Desert I Brou- 93
Tandis qu'à belles dents le nord 94
While with Appetite the North 95
Les terres la pierre la mousse 96
The Lands the Rock the Moss 97
Je suis une auto louée vouée 98
I Am a Rented Car Meant for 99
Passe un train-scie polychrome 100
A Train-Saw Polychrome Passes 101

Interview with Francis Catalano by Antonio D'Alfonso 103

INDEX

Je vais le faire apparaître
Ce qui est sous terre
Même si je dois l'exposer à la lumière.
Poème Chippewa

Quel – l'Amérique? – est l'immense vaisseau
porté sur le charroi de la mer?
Paul Chamberland

*I will make appear
That which is under the earth
Even if I have to expose it to the light.*
                    Chippewa poem

*What – America? – is the immense vessel
carried on the sea's chariot?*
                    Paul Chamberland

Amérique terre archaïque
sable sans sablier
Amérique du Nord Amérique du Nom
fragment de Pangée qui avance où s'étalent
ses pierres lentement
scellée à un secret lithique la Laurentia déroule
son granit convoyeur d'elle-même
qu'éventre le dos des océans
par l'ajour d'un casse-tête les yeux plissés je scrute
le continent qui se démantèle
dérive à l'emporte-pièce c'est un charroi
à plat ventre à outrance
basalte grinçant puisque raclé à fond
c'est une infra-amérique et son nord plonge
cap premier dans l'équateur
encastrements au modelé des gerbes minérales
plaque inféodée à son hésitante marche
nuptiale martiale tels les os
d'un crâne fracturé dont les cals
s'ajustent s'adjoignent poussent
– à la vitesse des cheveux
sur la tête abîmée d'un convalescent

America archaic earth
sand without sandglass
North America Named America
Pangee fragment that advances where slowly
its stones spread
sealed to a lithic secret the Laurentia unrolls
its own granite conveyor
that disembowels oceans' backs
through the openwork of a puzzle eyes squinting I
    scrutinise
the continent dismantling itself
drifting incisively it's a chariot
flat on its face excessive
grating basalt since it's scraped to the core
it's an infra-America and its North plunges
cape first into the equator
flush fitting as modelled by mineral sheaves
slabs pledged to its hesitant
nuptial martial march like bones
from a fractured skull whose calluses
adjust adjoin push
– at the speed of hairs
on the damaged head of a convalescent

Ici j'assiste dans toute sa grâce
à une surrection spontanée de montagnes
là un volcan sous pression se déconnecte
de sa cheminée ardente
bientôt en une envolée en rase-mottes d'archéoptéryx
l'un d'eux fixera sur sa pupille
tout le global et l'invisible
de ce paysage sans relief cerclé de carbone
– déjà enclin à rajeunir
en une nanoseconde la lumière fait le croquis
d'une fleur qu'elle glisse en silence
sous les feuilletages d'une falaise
à forme de quartz le hasard
ravalé par les mégapoles dans les géodes
en couches le continent travaille à mettre bas
la pierre et la fièvre la bouche
des cratères éructe une mémoire lapis-lazuli
en gésine l'océan l'est aussi
je ne vois pas l'homme mais ses arêtes pulvérisées
s'amonceler sur les hauts fonds
blanches comme neige tomber
parmi les algues bleues

Here I assist in all its glory
at a spontaneous upheaval of mountains
there a volcano disconnects under pressure
from its ardent chimney
soon in a flight of hedge-hopping archaeopteryx
one of them will fix on its pupil
all the global and invisible
of this flat landscape encircled by carbon
– already inclined to rejuvenate
in a nanosecond the light sketches
a flower that it slips silently
under a leafy cliff
shaped like quartz chance
restored by the megalopolis in the geodes
in layers the continent works to give birth
to stone and fever the mouth
of craters burps a lapis-lazuli memory
in labour also the ocean
I do not see man but its pulverised ridges
drift in the shallows
white like falling snow
among blue algae

Laurentia tapie sous l'Amérique
je rapplique par la contenance ocre de tes plages
les courbes giboyeuses d'un oscillogramme
pour constater ô gothique forêt
combien les Laurentides t'évoquent encore et toujours
le temps d'une fulminante saison
s'est défroissé le calque de tes lacs
revenant inlassable ectoplasme fugace
l'eau reflète l'obstination du glacier
à secouer les montagnes au bout de leurs chaînes
– regarde au fond du cratère
le météorite se rappeler les tremblements de lune
regarde cela qui des lacs remonte en touffe à la surface
traçant à la pointe sèche des pilotis mous
tes socles lacunaires Laurentia
sitôt qu'ils s'exondent t'aimantent
à mesure qu'elle renonce aux glaces
ta mémoire s'égoutte

Laurentia crouched under America
I return by the ochre countenance of your beaches
the abundant curves of an oscilloscope
to notice oh gothic forest
how Laurentians remember you again and again
the duration of a thunderous season
has smoothed out the traces of your lakes
reverting to tireless fleeting ectoplasm
the water reflects the glacier's obstinacy
to shake the mountains on the ends of their chains
– look in the bottom of the crater
the meteorite recalls the moon's tremors
look what the lakes raise to the surface in clumps
drawing with the dry points of pliant stilts
your deficient platforms Laurentia
as soon as they reach dry land they magnetize you
as they relinquish ice so too
your memory drips away

Accroupi au bord de l'abîme je m'imagine
un monde réversible où le temps
viendrait à sa fin comme un film passant à l'envers
on verrait Colomb Cabot Cortès Cartier Champlain
copyright en main faire machine arrière
les Incas peut-être découvrir l'Europe
l'Homo Laurentientis traqué par des bêtes immaculées
aller à reculons par une Béringie en fleurs
on verrait les arbres choir à côté de leurs fruits
la pluie réintégrer les cumulus déshydratés
de bas en haut à torrent
dans la mire de la préhistoire l'homme surgit
mais c'est l'histoire qui l'atteint
en plein cœur d'où se déverse le réversible
je le regarde fuir le passé le passé
fuir de lui par un trou béant dans sa poitrine
il s'éloigne du mal de lui-même
qui passe guérir quérir périr
sont sa seule rémission
– car avant d'être remède l'Amérique
était un ready made

Crouched by the side of the abyss I imagine
a reversible world for me where time
would reach its end like a film shown backwards
we'd see Columbus Cabot Cortes Cartier Champlain
copyright in hand rewind
the Incas perhaps discover Europe
Homo Laurentientis tracked by immaculate beasts
move backwards on Beringia in flower
we'd see trees drop next to their fruits
the rain reintegrating the dehydrated cumulus
in torrents from the bottom up
from the cross-hairs of prehistoric times man surges
    forth
but it's history that hits him
straight through the heart where the reversible pours
    out
I watch him flee the past the past
flee from him by a gaping hole in his chest
he distances himself from his own ills
that pass to healing seeking perishing
these his only remission
– for before becoming remedy America
was a "ready-made"

L'ombre d'un cervidé m'appâte
jusqu'à la constriction crépitante des glaces
quoi d'autre devrais-je m'acharner
à trimballer sur le dos quels autres fagots d'éclisses
à quoi devrais-je encore me hasarder
le Nord-Ouest si bien logé sous l'hypophyse
marcher longtemps fort longtemps
à bout de forces par-dessus mers et mondes
enjamber détroits atolls caps cordillères
je suis transi je suis une passoire pour le froid
je souffle dans le cou de l'homme
– la lune est un œil incrusté dans le nul
à peine suit-il mon odyssée à travers sa cataracte
l'inlandsis m'éblouit puis m'opacifie
aussi absent que sibérien je disparais en des zigzags
arctiques réapparais sur les aléoutiennes
parmi les profils prognathes
éclat de silex j'avance d'un pas muet
un milliard d'autres à venir narguent l'arc du fémur
pleine bouche de cavernes je viens
ma semence sourdant comme un jet figé
pour embrasser le rire à écailles
que l'horizon affiche

The shadow of a deer lures me in
as far as the crackling constriction of ice
what else should I slave away at
carrying some more bundles of sticks on my back
what else should I try my luck at
the North-West is so well housed under the pituitary gland
walking a long time a very long time
exhausted over seas and worlds
straddling straits atolls capes cordillera
I am chilled I am a sieve for the cold
I blow down the neck of man
– the moon is an eye incrusted in the void
it just manages to follow my odyssey through its cataract
the ice sheet dazzles me then dulls me
as absent as Siberian I disappear in arctic
zigzags reappear on the Aleutians
among prognathic profiles
flint slivers I advance with silent steps
a billion others to come taunt the femur arc
mouth full of caverns I come
my spurting seed a fixed jet
for kissing the scaly laugh
posted on the horizon

Il neigeait doucement
sur la plaque continentale
comme il avait neigé durant tout l'âge de pierre
une simple chiquenaude sur l'ADN
m'entraîna vers le tourniquet des errances
cette chute dans l'Animal farouche
c'est l'Ours et l'Étoile polaires embrasés
– c'est encore un gouffre noir
s'ouvrant sur un gouffre blanc
plusieurs ciels empalés dans la nuque
parvenir au triangle de l'Ungava tandis que le climat
un à un enlève ses châles
les glaces sans ardeur retournent à l'eau
là seulement là découvrir en un tapotement
de la paume sur les lèvres
que du fond du gosier peut naître
un cri plus pur que l'hameçon

It was gently snowing
on the continental plate
like it had snowed during the entire stone age
a simple blip on the DNA
drew me towards the tourniquet of nomadism
this fall into the fierce Animal
it's the Bear and Star poles ablaze
– it's another black hole
opening onto a white hole
several skies impaled in the neck
reach the Ungava triangle while the climate
removes its shawls one by one
the ice lacking fervour returns to water
there only there to discover by a tap
of a palm on the lips
that from the depths of a throat may rise
a cry purer than the hook

Des visages ravinés sombrent çà et là
dans l'opaque poudrerie
je marche face au vent moi l'Esquimau-Aléoute
dont le devenir est immobile
cheveux éclaboussez tels des flocons de quartz
au contact de cette brise temporisatrice
écartez-vous de mon faciès bleui
prête-nom d'une étoile avec ma besace
je prends mes distances du sous-ordre des simiens
tant de sons pour décrire la neige
pas un seul pour dire qui je suis
en ce no man's land dévaler migrer chuter
– nomade jusqu'au plus secret nævus sur la peau
aller de l'avant toujours de l'avant
tournant ma langue de glace
dos à la bourrasque je presse le pas vers la mer
des Tchouktches où d'essentiels clivages sévissent
poussière dans l'œil sans iris de la lune voilà
dans quel blanc je me trouve

Furrowed faces slump here and there
in the opaque powder snow
I walk face to the wind me Eskimo-Aleut
whose future is immobile
hair spattered like flakes of quartz
in contact with this intransient breeze
move away from my bluish features
borrowed name of a star with my pouch
I keep my distance from the lower order of the Simians
so many sounds to describe snow
not a single one to say who I am
in this no man's land hurtle migrate fall
– nomad in the most secret nevus on the skin
moving forward always forward
turning my tongue to ice
back to the gusts I hurry on towards
the Tchotchkes sea where essential divides vent
dust into the iris-less eye of the moon this is
the white place I am in

Le pôle vie le pôle mort entre les deux dériver
il y a les vieillards à leurs harangues
des glaçons se sont ficelés
puis il y a les nouveaux-nés qu'on emmitoufle
au creux des naganes des femmes
d'une rive à l'autre Béring fait pression
les champs magnétiques mangent mes yeux
rétractés dans le regard
la course du gibier d'hier
revisite cette constellation en forme de casserole
les mots sont trapus bancals je les laisse aller outre
– venant de nulle part je ne vais nulle part
au groupe j'évoque une terre promise
au réchauffement un pays
d'abondance de danses de bonds de cerfs
devant l'étendue de mes paraboles
je me fais petit passe par l'étroit d'un son
si bien que les vieillards croient entendre
voler une hâtive drosophile
petits manchots mystiques les enfants battent
éperdument des mains

The pole alive the pole dead between the two drifting
there are old men ranting
icicles are tied
then there are the new born wrapped up
in the crux of women's naganes
from one bank to the other Bering presses
magnetic fields eat my eyes
retracted from sight
yesterday's hunt for game
revisits this constellation in the shape of a saucepan
words are squat rickety I leave them be
– coming from nowhere I am going nowhere
to the group I evoke a promised land
warming a country
abundant with the dances of leaping stags
before the extent of my parables
I make myself small pass through the narrowness
    of a sound
so well that the old men believe they hear
flying a hasty drosophilia
small mystic penguins the children
madly clap their hands

Tenace race de Siam perdure
continue d'enfanter sur la solidité des lacs vermillons
traque l'Animal avec sa croupe inusitée
et dépèce-le équitablement
quant aux crânes de l'homme sous le permafrost
ils feront les frais d'un paléontologue à venir
dans mon visage la neige tournoie – folle
le vent je le sens me reporte
à plus tard à plus loin ses racines abreuvées
au souffle du sud fossile
ici les glaces glissent au large précis
c'est une blouse blanche lâche
le Nord se déboîte éperon après éperon
je me surprends à contempler cela
quand d'étranges oiseaux aquatiques s'adonnent
à faire des vrilles sur mon front
serti d'une mer étale

Tenacious race of Siam endures
continues to raise children on the solid vermillion
 lakes
trails the Animal with its unused croup
and cuts it up fairly
as for the skulls of man under the permafrost
they will pay the price of a palaeontologist to come
in my face the snow swirls – folly
the wind I feel it carry me forward
in time and place its roots watered
by the breath of the south fossil
here ice blocks slide out to precise open seas
it's a loose white blouse
the North dislodges spur after spur
I surprise myself contemplating that
when strange aquatic birds devote themselves
to making spirals on my forehead
set in a sprawling sea

Marcher et inventer font un
ainsi va la formule du progrès en ces parallèles
qui dit stagner dit pourrir
– ce chien qui dort est-il toujours autorisé à s'appeler
 un chien
l'atteler à l'amorce osseuse d'un traîneau
puis glisser sur ces terres sans balises ni repères
privées de verticalité glisser
sous un soleil jamais couché jamais levé
énigmatique vitesse aux pôles
en moins de temps plus d'espace blanc
glisser glisser bon an mal an certains
poursuivent cette topographie épicée de rennes
d'autres lancent leur parka alors tant pis
comme les planètes planent
la Terre erre les cailloux caillent
je lâche au loin le chien que j'ai au ventre
et le voilà au cœur de la taïga
à lécher les plaies des baies pendillant aux arbustes
puisqu'il est l'os l'homme se rapproche
à l'orient de rien des oies sauvages s'éclatent
il y aurait cinq lacs qui décongèlent
une forêt de billots debout on ne glisse plus
même avant d'y être entré
l'homme n'est pas sorti du bois

Walking and inventing are one and the same
so says the formula for progress in these parallels
he who stagnates rots
– this sleeping dog is it authorized to still be called
    a dog
harnessed to the bony section of a sledge
then sliding on these lands without signposts
    or landmarks
deprived of verticality sliding
under a sun never set never risen
enigmatic speed at the poles
in less time more white space
sliding sliding year in year out certain ones
follow this topography spiced with reindeer
others launch their parka so tough luck
as planets patrol
the Earth errs the gravel gravitates
I leave far behind the dog in my stomach
and there it is in the heart of the taiga
licking wounded berries hanging from bushes
because he is bone man moves closer
to the east of nothingness wild geese break out
there could be five lakes thawing
a forest of upright stumps we slide no more
even before entering there
man is not out of the woods yet

ROMAMOR

*Jouir une seule minute de vie initiale
je cherche un pays innocent.*
                    Giuseppe Ungaretti

*To possess a single minute of initial life
I search for an innocent country*
                    Giuseppe Ungaretti

Splendeur des yeux dessillés
qui à l'obscurité s'habituent,
il règne dans cette pièce une grandiose
nuit d'encre, j'y trempe mes mots
jusqu'à la racine afin
que les objets familiers graduellement
se hissent, réintègrent leur place,
tremblants et friables
comme le matériel d'une archéologie
mentale, du silence remué.

Splendour of eyes unsealed
that become used to darkness,
there reigns in this room a grandiose
inky night, I dip my words into it
down to the roots so
that familiar objects gradually
pull themselves up, regain their place,
trembling and crumbly
like the material of a mental
archaeology, of stirred silence.

En filigrane du rêve, qui va là?
À défaut de comparaître au for intérieur
est-ce l'amour, la mort
par procuration ou est-ce ton ombre
s'agitant sous un masque clair?
Mais en soulevant les voilures du lit
j'ai vu gésir mon absence:
ni là, ni ici, ni partout ailleurs.

In the haziness of a dream, who goes there?
By failing to appear deep within
is this love, death
by proxy or is it your shadow
shaking beneath a clear mask?
But on lifting the bed's canopy
I saw my absence lying:
not there, not here, nor anywhere else.

Depuis le rectangle de la chambrette
j'observe la poussière
de la fenêtre se déposer,
ensevelir mes pieds dessinés sur le marbre.
Les ruines sont ce qu'elles sont :
d'hier et d'aujourd'hui, miennes.

From the rectangle of the small bedroom
I observe the dust
from the window deposit itself,
burying my feet outlined on the marble.
The ruins are what they are:
of yesterdays and todays, mine.

Derrière les murs il est des murs
et derrière encore
un réseau d'aqueducs anciens.
Durant la nuit l'eau a dormi,
détenu croupissant
écroué dans des coudes et des raccords.
J'ai ouvert le robinet, levier
libérateur et avec les mains mises en coquille,
ses dix fossiles pétrifiés,
j'ai recueilli le jet, arrose
le visage qui a éclos.

Behind the walls are walls
and further behind still
a network of ancient aqueducts.
During the night water has slept,
held stagnant
imprisoned in bends and joints.
I opened the tap, liberating
lever and with my hands cupped,
their ten fossils petrified,
I welcomed the stream, sprinkling
my face that blossomed.

Vus d'en bas les toits de tuiles
incurvées ont l'aspect flou
du homard au fond de l'eau, sa vulnérabilité,
sa couleur terre cuite,
d'ici on dirait qu'au moindre péril
ce qui abrite s'abrite aussi.
Au pied de la fixité, au pas des portails,
les antennules les voir
courber, plier, tendre dans l'onde
sens dessus dessous
alors qu'à l'aube des premières émissions
les antennes télé se frôlent
là-haut sur des toitures.

Seen from below the curved tiled roofs
have the fuzzy appearance
of a lobster in the bottom of the water,
    its vulnerability,
its baked earth colour,
from here we'd say that at the slightest danger
that which gives shelter also takes shelter.
At the foot of fixity, on the steps of gateways,
tiny antennae see them
bending, folding, tender in the wave
upside down
while at the dawn of the first programmes
the television aerials brush against each other
up there on the rooftops.

Lire un livre tel l'aruspice
interprète les entrailles d'un rossignol
puis prendre les augures.
Un livre ouvert, tourner ses ailes
pour voir le temps qu'il fera,
lecture coupée du monde
et des prévisions météorologiques.

Read a book like an aruspice
interpret the innards of a nightingale
then take the predictions.
An open book, turning its wings
to see what the weather will be,
reading cut off from the world
and meteorological forecasts.

Un touriste avance, avance
en sens inverse un détachement
de jeunes tziganes,
yankees, pickpocket aguerris,
une dent en or et pourvus
des rabats d'une boîte en carton.
Gisant, gitans, ce sont des signes
de rue : le futur, tôt
ou tard les romanichels le chiperont
au touriste, dans la poche
intérieure du veston, sa doublure,
les coutures décousues.
Poème et bohème dérobés.

A tourist advances, advances
in the opposite direction a detachment
of young gypsies,
yankees, battle-hardened pickpockets,
a gold tooth and armed
with flaps from a cardboard box.
Lying, gypsies, these are the signs
of the street: the future, sooner
or later these Romanis will pinch it
from the tourist, in the jacket's
inside pocket, its lining,
seams unpicked.
Poems and bohemians robbed.

D'ici part tout le pavé romain
composé de sanpietrini, pierres non plus
superposées, juxtaposées,
mais étalées et imbriquées au sol.
Routes, voies, avenues,
tout est question d'étendre, de tentacules
et le soir lorsqu'il pleut
les sanpietrini
deviennent une mue de serpent,
gisante, luisante, glissante,
noires petites pierres saintes,
mosaïque rustique
où le pied par une venelle
prend son envol.

From here all the Roman cobblestones leave
composed of sanpietrini, stones neither
superposed, juxtaposed,
but interlocked and overlapping on the ground.
Roads, lanes, avenues,
all is a question of stretching out, of tentacles
and the evening when it rains
the sanpietrini
become a serpent's sloughing skin,
slipping, shining, sliding,
small black saintly stones,
rustic mosaic
where feet in an alley
take flight.

. . . la langue est un moyen de s'entendre indispensable, mais sans direction, et donc utilisable arbitrairement, un moyen aussi indifférent qu'un moyen de transport en commun, tel un tramway, où n'importe qui monte et descend.
Martin Heidegger

À l'arrêt j'attends, muet
que s'immobilise une phrase pour y monter.
Je sors d'un long mutisme.
Sitôt timbré mon ticket j'accorde
mon souffle à celui des autres.
Intérieurement, tout parle : les journaux lus,
la pub dont nul ne fait plus cas,
l'art des regards, furtifs, amendés ou insistants.
Les choses sortent lentement de leur narcose,
la mémoire de son trou.
Vont jusqu'à murmurer les habits des usagers.
Mais sur leur visage, que dalle :
lignes, tangentes, sinus d'un graphique.
Tout en oscillant, j'avance ceci
ou cela : que les idées
piétinent, ne vont nulle part,
langue pleine à craquer.
Attendu que les paroles s'envolent
par des systèmes de transport en commun,
je préfère de loin descendre
au prochain arrêt
pour marcher seul dans l'imprimé.

> *... that the language in general is worn out and used up – an indispensable but masterless means of communication that may be used as one pleases, as indifferent as a means of public transport, as a street car which everyone rides in.*
>
> Martin Heidegger

At the bus stop I wait, mute
that a phrase immobilizes itself to step on it.
I'm emerging from a long silence.
As soon as my ticket has been stamped I match
my breathing to that of the others.
Internally, everything speaks: papers read,
ads that no one bothers with,
the art of looking, furtive, modified or insistent.
Things slowly emerge from their narcosis,
the memory from its hole.
Go as far as murmuring the passengers' clothes.
But on their faces, damn all:
lines, tangents, sinus on a graph.
Everything swaying, I put forward this
or that: that the ideas
mark time, go nowhere,
tongue ready to burst.
Seeing that words fly off
through public transport systems,
I much prefer to get off
at the next stop
to walk alone among the printed matter.

Adolescent, mes rêves les plus chers
avaient forme de nuage.
À présent, ce sont de réels cirrostratus.
Toujours je cours derrière mes rêves
qui fuient, poussés dans le ciel
par de grands vents impitoyables,
je poursuis mes rêves
partis au loin argenter l'ouest.

Adolescent, my dearest dreams
were in the form of clouds.
Now, they are real cirrostratus.
Always I run after my dreams
that flee, pushed in the sky
by great unforgiving winds,
I follow my dreams
departed faraway to silver the west.

> *La lumière n'a pas de langue,*
> *elle est tout œil.*
>
> John Donne

Après un mois d'averses,
quand rapplique le soleil comme un seigneur
sur son fief, on dirait
le monde surexposé, les choses
par leur avers rejaillir
d'un éclat qu'on ne leur connaissait pas
et où que l'on soit, que l'on aille
la lumière met des bâtons,
fait trébucher, on tombe, se relève
le soleil toujours dans les yeux.

> *Light hath no tongue,*
> *but is all eye.*
>
> John Donne

After a month of showers,
when the sun returns like a lord
over his fiefdom, it seems
the world is overexposed, things
by their obverse side burst again
with a brilliance unknown to us
and wherever we are, wherever we go
the light puts out sticks,
makes us trip, fall, get up
the sun still in our eyes.

Le front plaqué au ciel je traverse
place de la Rotonde regardant à contre-courant
passer un vol de pigeons.
Ce vol, ces ailes, toute cette légèreté
impressionnée en négatif à bout d'œil.
Oui c'est majestueux
voir un tournoiement ainsi se déplacer
sur un axe aérien
en de telles flopées de battements cardiaques,
croix qui fendent l'air suivant
une logique, qui se multiplient,
commutent, grisent le sillage bleu ciel
et qui voient tout défiler
comme un film que l'on visionnerait
couché sur le ventre.

My forehead stuck against the sky I cross
Rotunda square watching in contra flow
a flock of pigeons fly by.
This flight, these wings, all this lightness
imprinted in negative on the edge of my eye.
Yes it's majestic
to see a swirling cloud move like that
on an aerial axis
in such a mass of heart beats,
crosses splitting the air following
some logic, multiplying,
switching, tingeing the sky blue trail grey
and seeing all parading past
like a film I'd view
lying on my front.

Les églises sont les tendons mystiques
d'une ville, leur corps
au repos et ce matin j'entre dans celui,
affaibli, échafaudé, de San Francesco
à Ripa à Trastevere.
Dans une chapelle, au fond
gît le marbre de Ludovica Albertoni.
Elle est là, blanche, étendue,
vouée à une calme félicité,
sa main droite offrant le sein, le pressant presque,
une invite à un amour licencieux.
M'approcher, glisser sur les plis
de sa robe, l'envie de lécher
le marbre, mordre,
moi, agent érosif de l'immuable.

Churches are the mystical tendons
of a town, their bodies
at rest and this morning I enter this one,
weakened, with scaffolding, San Francesco
a Ripa, Trastevere.
In a chapel, at the back
lies the marble of Ludovica Albertoni.
She's there, white, stretched out,
devoted to a calm felicity,
her right hand offering her breast, almost pressing it,
an invite to a licentious love.
I approach, slipping on the folds
of her dress, I want to lick
the marble, bite,
me, an erosive agent of the perpetual.

Sur l'échiquier, pré géométrique
truqué d'avance où ont le loisir de circuler
librement deux paires de fous,
je sème, ludique, la zizanie,
moi arlequin zigzaguant entre les figures.
Çà et là j'évince un cavalier
ou pulvérise un pion puis, emporté,
je fonds sur la Reine et l'étrenne.
Au galop, en diagonale cette fois
et tournant le dos à la plaine,
nous commençons à disparaître laissant derrière
une traînée de poudre
mais j'ai tout juste le temps, avec elle en selle,
avant que ne s'efface le jeu,
de passer sous un aqueduc, raser
ces murs à Assise,
gravir un pic et apercevoir,
inexpugnable, mathématique, sévère,
lot de tout joueur,
la Tour divinement crénelée
flanquée du même beffroi droit
où, blanc sur noir,
je peux enfin aimer ma Dame,
la prendre doucement avant
notre fatale disparition.
Sauvegarde et proclamation
de cette partie nulle.

On the chessboard, geometric field
fixed in advance where two pairs of fools have the time
to circulate freely,
I, playfully, stir up trouble,
me harlequin zigzagging between the pieces.
Here and there I unseat a knight
or pulverize a pawn then, carried away,
I swoop on the Queen and take her.
Galloping, diagonally this time
and turning my back to the plain,
we start to disappear leaving behind us
a trail of powder
but I've got just enough time, with her in the saddle,
before the game fades,
to pass under an aqueduct, hug
the walls of Assisi,
climb a peak and notice,
inexpungible, mathematical, severe,
every player's lot,
the Tower divinely crenelated
flanked by the same tall belfry
where, white on black,
I can at last love my Lady,
take her gently before
our fatal disappearance.
Safeguard and proclamation
of this drawn game.

Écrire un livre sur rien, absolument
que personne encore n'a écrit.
Rien qu'un livre, support
pour les pages et une couverture.
Ni rectangulaire ni carrée,
ni vivante ni morte, plaquette ou brique,
qu'une forme libre.
Pour cela, il faudrait s'aviser de vider
les mots, les évider, enlever
ce qu'il y a dedans qui leur donne
un poids et une inclinaison :
il faudrait réussir à détuber
des mots les choses, les euthanasier
faire la nuit sur les signes en leur injectant
une robuste dose de rien.
De cette opération, seul
demeurerait le visage de la mère, sourire
flottant dans l'apesanteur.

Write a book about nothing, absolutely
that no one has written yet.
Nothing but a book, support
for the pages and a cover.
Not rectangular nor square,
not alive nor dead, plaquette or pamphlet,
only a free form.
For that, it is necessary to dare emptying
words, hollowing them out, taking out
what inside of them gives them
weight and an inclination:
it is necessary to successfully extract
the words from the things, euthanize them
bring the night to fall upon the signs by injecting
   them with
a robust dose of nothing.
From this operation, only
the mother's face will remain, a smile
floating in weightlessness.

Clore les yeux à double tour,
le corps tourné vers l'intérieur et voir
l'immobilité du monde,
idéale, à l'affût, prête à croquer
la scène d'un frugal retour aux sources.
Se portraiture enfin la joie:
un kaki mûr, trop mûr pour figurer
dans un plat de fruits.

Lock your eyes tight,
your body turned inwards and see
the world's immobility,
ideal, alert, ready to bite into
the scene of a frugal return to basics.
Its portrait finally joyful:
a ripe persimmon, too ripe to be placed
in a fruit bowl.

Au tintement des cloches,
le risque d'écarquillement que court
mon cœur fêlé est grand.
Défenestrée, soufflée, mon âme
longe des murs sujets
à la pérennité m'accompagnant
jusqu'où la lumière taille.

With the pealing of the bells,
the risk of wide-eyed wonder that runs through
my cracked heart is great.
Defenestrated, breathless, my soul
hugs the walls subject
to the permanence accompanying me
to where the light severs.

Les idées, concepts ou images
reflètent la profondeur, l'usure même
des sites archéologiques,
cavités, caries,
dents malades à extraire ou bien à obturer.
Aussi, l'impression
de voir dans les mots un peloton de touristes
prenant en photo ces choses
qu'ils cerclent et qu'ils ont tout autour.
Au couchant, en groupe
ils se retirent, refluent, retraitent
vers leur hôtel, illuminés
par ce qui fut un jour
et n'est plus, ils retournent
à leur trou comme une langue par instinct
cherche dans la bouche
la cassure de la dent.
La nuit on donne ces sites aux chats.

Ideas, concepts or images
reflect the depth, the wear and tear
of archaeological sites,
cavities, holes,
bad teeth to be extracted or filled.
Also, the impression
to see in words a pack of tourists
taking photos of those things
that they surround and that are all around them.
At night, in a group
they retire, replete, retreat
to their hotel, illuminated
by the day that has passed
and is no more, they return
to their holes like a tongue instinctively
searches out in its mouth
the broken tooth.
At night these sites are given over to cats.

Brunissent le soir les pastels de la ville
et lorsqu'on avance d'arrache-pas
vers l'ambrejaune crépusculaire,
on dirait que Rome se ferme
comme ces livres animés, à trois dimensions,
quand le décor replie ses formes,
quand le relief retourne au calme plat
et se croyant au centre
quand le monde se reploie sur soi,
on rentre la tête sous l'arc
de Constantin ou le Colisée, enfin
enclin à l'autoscopie.
Là, inclut dans l'Urbs et l'incluant,
la figure dans les empans,
on pense que,
au lieu d'être celui-ci ou celui-là,
on est son être
on est son être à sa place.

Tingeing brown the town's evening pastels
and when we advance hurriedly
towards the amber-yellow twilight
it seems that Rome is closing
like those three dimensional books,
where the scenery folds back down,
where the contours return to a calm flatness
believing themselves to be at the centre
when the world folds in on itself,
our heads pulled in under the arch of
Constantine or the Coliseum, at last
ready for an inner scan.
There, included in the Urbs and including it,
our face in our hands,
we think that,
instead of being this or that one,
we are our self
we are our self in our place.

WHERE SPACES GLOW

L'organe du langage, c'est la main.
                               Valère Novarina

Monde, sois, et sois bon;
existe bonnement,
fais que, cherche à, tends à, dis-moi tout...
                               Andrea Zanzotto

The organ of language is the hand.
                    Valère Novarina

World be, and be good;
Behave nicely,
See to it that, try to, aim at, tell me all . . .
                    Andrea Zanzotto

LE CIEL EN PETITES COUPURES À PLATES
coutures que tranche
la ligne-hache des montagnes
acérées arides
retailles de papier volt-
igeant bleu par-
delà les pics ocres les
socles esthétiques
avions de chasse furtifs dissimulés
dans les pétroglyphes
ici-bas un noyau de pêche irréel
roule irrégulier irradié
sur la voie carrossable chauf-
fée par les pneus les nœuds
par le peu d'âme le trop plein
de rien dans les réservoirs
d'essence et les
réserves d'indiens :

(Crépuscule du matin)

THE SKY IN LITTLE SLICES WITH FLAT
seams that cut
the angular-line mountains
parched sharpened
strips of paper swirl-
ing blue abo-
ve the ochre peaks the
aesthetic socle
furtive fighter jets hidden
in the petroglyphs
here below an unreal peach stone
rolls irregular irradiated
on the chassis bearing lane heat-
ed by tires the knots
by the bit of soul overfull
with nothingness in the reservoirs
of gasoline and the
Indian reserves:

(Morning twilight)

ARIZ ARIAS ARIENS ARIZONA
zona arida rides sur le neck
cactus posé sur le meuble en teck
le soleil ses airs de Hopi
la lune dans l'œil du cowboy
« oyé oyé » l'Arizona est une
ligne cette ligne pure
d'un pont d'une highway
d'un viaduc qu'empalent les nopals
que traversent les mœurs
des Navajos des nævi sur la peau
des halos des niveaux
vu que dedans gère l'intérieur le
réfrigère mais à la fin
c'est moi – ou est-ce une image de moi? –
qui me figure le paysage a-
vec des aigles safran
ils tournent dans le vert-mousse
au-dessus de la crevasse de la
grande ride Arizona de la
zone A de l'abc tout
l'Az enroulé :

(Plaques minéaralogiques)

ARIZ ARIAS ARIENS ARIZONA
zona arida wrinkles on the neck
cactus sitting on the teak table
the sun with its Hopi ways
the moon in the cowboy's eye
"oyé oyé" Arizona is a
line this pure line
of a bridge of a highway
of a viaduct that spears the nopals
that travels through the morals
of Navajos naevi on their skin
halos of tiers
viewed that within govern the interior
refrigerate it but in the end
it's me – or is it a picture of me? –
that imagines the landscape wi-
th saffron eagles
that turn in the moss-green
above the crevice of the
large crow's foot Arizona from
the A zone of the abc all
the A to Zs wrapped up:

(Mineralogical plates)

LE BLANC VIN L'HERBE
vert-bouteille le roc
les ocres les profils ogres
aigle jaune safran buvant
une courbe de soleil
survole
des coyotes hot
des poissons frétillent et
les lacs Apache et Roosevelt
le blanc vin blond
dans le verre tournoie verdoie
le même aigle jaune safran
fonce vers le nihil le vi-
de serres serrées boucle
bouclée un lézard pé-
trifié dans l'idem
une pluie de proies crochu
le bec-cible et branchu et
fourchu et fichu
Arizona as is que fend
un pionnier has been
pioche à hauteur de
joue du pion
du grand chef du cavalier
du roi et mat et regarde
et prend garde
et cætera :   (Échec et mat)

THE WHITE WINE THE GRASS
bottle-green the rock
the ochres the ogres profiles
saffron yellow eagle drinking
an arc of sun
flies above
hot coyotes
fish wriggle and
the Apache and Roosevelt lakes
the white wine blonde
in a glass turns verdant
the same yellow saffron eagle
swoops towards the nihil emp-
ties it claws clawing circle
encircling a lizard pe-
trified in the idem
a rain of prey hooked
the target-beak and branched and
forked and done for
Arizona as is that splits
a has been pioneer
pickaxe at cheek
level of a pawn
a great chief a knight
king and checkmate and watches
and watches out
et cetera: (Checkmate)

SI LE SOLEIL EST L'OEUF LA TERRE (JE M'EN VEUX)
est le rond du poêle
une spirale aspire les mots
les casse il convient avant
le silence de casser la coquille
des mots leur substance
s'étale alors comme la mer
les mots les jaunes le soleil
s'étalent aussi cuire
sur le vieux rond de poêle en spirale
altitude zéro Terre
degré absolu
faisant en sorte que le poème reprenne
forme pour qu'il
redevienne blanc
silence d'avant
avant la bouche de l'uni-
vers :

(Au Waffle House)

IF THE SUN IS THE EGG THE EARTH (I BLAME MYSELF)
is the hotplate of the hob
a stove spiral sucks up words
breaks them it should be before
the silence breaks the shell
of words their substance
spreads like the sea
words yellow yolks the sun
spreads also cooks
on the old spiral surface element
altitude zero Earth
absolute degree
making it so that the poem takes
form to again
become white
silence before
before the mouth of the uni-
verse:

(At the Waffle House)

Tout est régi par l'éclair
Héraclite

L'APACHE TRAIL LA PAIX
la grande paix (on dit qu'elle s'achète)
avec énergie d'images
privés de couilles les cactus à candélabres
défendent leur aride espace leur
alcool leur système de refroidisse-
ment endo-végétatif
cactus-fréon petits bonhommes de chemin
bras en l'air caquet bas cactées gras
cependant qu'un éclair-aiguille zig-
zague dans le ciel bleu blanc
rouge pâle tel un aigle
safran en boucle tournoie
lentement et frappe
dans le nihil dans le mille
dans un nuage
de poussière :

(Antique surface)

> *Everything is directed by lightning*
> Heraclitus

THE APACHE TRAIL PEACE
great peace (it's said it can be bought)
with the energy of images
deprived of balls the candelabra cacti
defend their arid space their
alcohol their system of cool-
ing endo-vegetative
freon-cacti little men passing through
arms in the air low cackle fatty cacti
while a needle of lightning zig-
zags in a blue white sky
pale red like a saffron eagle
in a circle turns
slowly and strikes
in the nihil dead on target
in a cloud
of dust:

(Antique surface)

L'ŒUF LE BŒUF LA BOUFFE
Buffalo Bill Hopi colonisé
Apache assimilé
par la malbouffe le bœuf neuf
l'aigle safran et
le Navajo équarri
par ronald par le colonel
Buffalo Bill les tacos les Amérin-
diens désintéressés désindianisés
déhydratés en désintoxe
culture et culte ôtés
côtes levées colt braqué
sur la terre-tempe ac-
culés à rien acculturés par
l'œuf le bœuf bof la mal-
bouffe dans le désert-désir
à plat sous l'effet
du rabot sous l'effet
du Bulldozer Bill :

(Vers Monument Valley)

THE BULL'S-EYE THE BULL THE BILL
Buffalo Bill colonized Hopi
Apache assimilated
by the junk food the ground beef
the saffron eagle and
the Navajo squared off
by ronald by the colonel
Buffalo Bill the tacos of the Amerin-
dians disinterested de-indianized
dehydrated in detox
culture and cults cut
ribs lifted Colt pointed
at the earth-brow brou-
ght to nothing acculturated by
the bull's-eye, the bull, the junk
food in a desire-desert
flattened by the effect
of a plane under the effect
of Bulldozer Bill:

(Near Monument Valley)

THE WEST OUAIS OUI OUEST
où est l'est à l'ouest ouais
aller où l'ouest est
d'ici à san à Alex aller avec Alex
vers l'est aztèque ou
avec Lou vers l'ouest
le toit ouvrant le soleil dedans
à l'apex au Texaco
taches d'huile à l'est de l'es-
sence the west the best ouais
the east the beast at least
est estival est estimé est stoma-
cal et tests dans l'ouest
des amants sur la route
l'ouest oui et les ai-
mants yes yes yes :

(Road poem I)

THE WEST YEAH YES OUEST
where is east to the west yeah
going where west is
from here to san to Alex to go with Alex
towards the Aztec east or
with Wes towards the west
the roof opening the sun within
at the apex of Texaco
oil stains in the east of unlea-
ded gas the west is best yeah
the east the beast at least
east estival east esteemed east eat-
en and tests in the west
lovers on the road
west yes and the lo-
de stone yes yes yes:

(Road poem I)

DU PAINTED DESERT J'AI RAM-
ené des troncs d'arbres pé-
trifiés des maux de bloc en quantité
des cafards somptueux j'ai
vu des Navajos rouler en Camaro
passer en trombe j'ai vu
des pinacles nature des pins-up
de pierre des pick-up mal assurés
des éclairs en vésicules
et des éclairs-clics dans les tapis
j'ai écouté des tipis prendre racine j'ai
aperçu des arcs-en-
ciel arc-boutés et doubles
des montures sans cavalier
des monts de catlinite
des indiens Hopis réas-
phalter leurs rites heu-
reux des Apaches mordre la poussière
dans des Thunderbird modi-
fiées j'ai entendu des mormons
murmurer en rêve damer
le pion à des pion-
niers au nez aquilin :

(Road poem II)

FROM THE PAINTED DESERT I BROU-
ght some tree trunks pe-
trified blocks of ills in quantities
sumptuous cockroaches I
saw Navajos driving in Camaros
zooming past I saw
natural pinnacles pin-ups
of stone pick-ups under insured
and flashes of capillaries
and flashes-clicks in the carpets
I heard the tepees take root I
registered the rain-
bows arc-bound and double
mounts without riders
mounts of catlinite
Hopi Indians reas-
phalting their rites hap-
py Apaches biting the dust
in Thunderbirds modi-
fied I heard Mormons
murmuring in dreams checkmate
for pawns of pion-
eers with aquiline noses:

(Road Poem II)

TANDIS QU'À BELLES DENTS LE NORD
mord la queue bleu ciel de
l'animal voyageur le sud-rut
rampe tire sa langue bifide
au sud dru au sud dur
au south-mouth et au sud-out
rond comme le Nord
vu l'ivresse dans les soutes de l'Ou-
est sur les rives de l'infini
écrire de la po-asie plages du Pacifique
écrire de la porient de la poccident
po-hiémal et po-midi
écrire sur un point cardinal
« pommade et époxy » :

(Road poem III)

WHILE WITH APPETITE THE NORTH
bites the sky blue tail of
the travelling animal the south-rut
ramps sticks out its split tongue
at the dense south at the tense south
at south-mouth and south-out
tipsy like the North
seeing insobriety in the holds of the We-
st on the banks of eternity
write po-asie of Pacific shores
write of porient of poccident
po-hibernal and po-southerly
write on a cardinal point
"pomade and epoxy":

(Road Poem III)

LES TERRES LA PIERRE LA MOUSSE
les roses du désert les opun-
tias les tumbleweeds qui roulent
les nopals les saguaros
la blondeur du vert des papillons ar-
més de libre-arbitre par-
delà le pare-brise écran
papillons safran tels aigles safran
en vol plané grande amplitude les ailes
puis plongeant vers leur asile
dans la nature-fissure
pour rien le nihil l'idem
le thrill de voler l'Apa-
che Trail sous le gril au gaz solaire
pour la finitude de l'asphalte
routes chiffonnées ar-
rivées à leurs fins :

(Road poem IV)

THE LANDS THE ROCK THE MOSS
the desert roses the opun-
tias the tumbleweeds that roll
the nopals the saguaros
the blondness of green butterflies ar-
med with free-arbiter ov-
er the windscreen screen
saffron butterflies like saffron eagles
in gliding flight large ample wings
then plunging towards their sanctuary
in the nature-fissure
for nothing the nihil idem
the thrill of flying the Apa-
che Trail under the solar gas grill
for the finitude of the asphalt
roads crumpled get-
ting their own way:

(Road Poem IV)

JE SUIS UNE AUTO LOUÉE VOUÉE
au lave-auto auto-auto
faite pour rouler que
pour rouler auto
non à soi auto à tous que chacun con-
duit on pose sa signature
laisse la barre à d'autres
c'est comme la langue ça sent
le neuf mais c'est usagé
puis on monte puis on descend
on remet les clés au suivant
qui y va de sa conduite avec son
style son technolecte
langage illimité air climatisé
GPS lecteur CD pourvu qu'à
la remise du véhicule
les niveaux – du sens? des sens?
de la langue? –
soient les mêmes qu'au début
à moitié plein à moitié
vide peu importe
à moitié dans la
moiteur de l'été :

(La baie de San Diego)

I AM A RENTED CAR MEANT FOR
a car-wash car-car
made for driving only
for driving car
not your car for all for each dr-
iver places his signature
leaves the bar for others
it's like a tongue that senses
the new but it's used
then we get in then get out
we hand over the keys to the next one
who will drive in their
style their own technical
unlimited language air conditioning
GPS reader CD as long as when
the car's given back
the levels – of sense? of senses?
of language? –
are the same as in the beginning
half full half
empty doesn't half
matter in the
summer stickiness:

(San Diego Bay)

PASSE UN TRAIN-SCIE POLYCHROME
une file Malévitch de rectangles Kandinsky
le long d'un vers volumé-
trique de Sandburg
train-train locomotive nature morte vivante
imperturbable hache inex-
orable hachis de cailloutis
moteurs à combustion explosion du roc
érosion du corps et de
l'âme siècles attachés un à un au
mouvement sans frein sans
entrain vers le programme-
progrès sous la fourchette-
assiette surtout surtout
bonnes bises aux bisons :

(Crépuscule du soir)

A TRAIN-SAW POLYCHROME PASSES
a long Malevich line of Kandinsky rectangles
the length of a volume-
tric verse by Sandburg
train-train locomotive still life living
imperturbable axe inex-
orable crushed gravel
combustion motors explosion of rock
erosion of body and
soul centuries attached one by one to
movement without brakes without
drive towards the programme-
progress under the fork-
plate especially especially
super smackers to the bison:

(Evening twilight)

INTERVIEW WITH FRANCIS CATALANO

ANTONIO D'ALFONSO

ANTONIO D'ALFONSO: Do you see stylistic, philosophical and ideological differences between your first literary adventures and this recent novelistic experience *On achève parfois ses romans en Italie?*

FRANCIS CATALANO: I started to write my first poems aged fifteen and to be published in serious or specialised reviews at nineteen. For me, *Quêtes* was a decisive step in my young writing career. With the text called "Scènes" (in my mind this title also suggested the Seine, and consequently my belonging to a linguistic group), I discovered my Italianism. In a way, I became symbolically Italian the day of that publication in 1983. I discovered the futurist movement, the skill involved in writing manifestos, how to do public readings, and to provoke. I was discovering my roots; this was the point of my text. I became Italian thanks to literature.

The novel that I have just published puts on the "stage" the student I was thirty years ago and who was off to continue his studies in Rome, experience adventures in Italy, while his grant lasted. It is certain that this tale gravitates around a quest for identity. But my style has not changed. I believe that one's style doesn't change: it's the stylus, the pen that plumbs the depths. And what is in the depths doesn't change.

In my novel I also provoke, I discover my roots, I strip myself bare. It's a very personal tale. There are several layers within the text. Certain are from 1986, others from 2008. It's a text which is an image of a country like Italy, with layers of time and history running through it. Life is like a novel. Each person has a story, his story. And the more we search, scratch the surface, the more likely we are to discover things beneath. That was my way of working. I let time settle within my story. That's the reason I chose this title for my novel.

ANTONIO D'ALFONSO: It seems to me that the question of identity is never simple for you. Even though it is based on a linguistic stance, more or less, the identity that calls to you is more fragmentary than linear. Isn't that a paradox?

FRANCIS CATALANO: Yes, paradoxes know all about me. We are up to our necks in paradoxes. Look what is happening in Italy. The Pope has resigned and Berlusconi is trying to hang onto power. Shouldn't it be the other way round? *(Laughter.)*

On a more serious note, I think that my Italianism is more schizoid (the root of *schizo* being "scission") than paradoxical, because of the language. I always find myself a stranger when faced with a language, whatever it may be – French, my maternal tongue or Italian, my father's language that I learnt at a later age.

I think that a writer should be a stranger to his own language. Also, before being born and even at birth, language is external to us. Afterwards we interiorize it. It shapes and forms us. But in the beginning, all language is imposed on us. In fact, it's the territory that imposes its language. The language talks to "us" about the place where it develops. Language is viral.

According to me, a writer is someone who, when s/he writes, recreates that state of initial wonder when faced with language, a certain word here that seems uncommon, or a certain phrasing there that says how beautiful and strange it can be. Writing is a solitary activity. To write is to isolate oneself from one world to enter another. Proust already confessed in *Contre Sainte-Beuve:* "Beautiful books are written in a sort of foreign language." That's why Rimbaud doesn't translate well. His oeuvre seems to have been written in this "sort of foreign language."

ANTONIO D'ALFONSO: Why this sudden move to writing a novel? Talk to us about the stylistic differences between writing a poem and a narrative text.

FRANCIS CATALANO: When I left for Rome in 1986 I had stopped writing. I had exhausted my resources, I had become blasé and I had nothing more to say. Then, Italy gave me back my taste for writing. I wrote everywhere. In restaurants, in bars, buses, during my university lectures, on trains. I lived through a sort of personal, internal rebirth.

When I decided to make a book out of all these small texts that I'd written as if outside of myself, I needed to assemble and order my writing. Time became the organising element in my novel. It represents the linear aspect (my novel is effectively chronological).

Writing poetry is more to do with space: space on the page, in the form and it is instant. Poems are dazzling like lightning. In a story, a narration, it is time that is important, that comes into play. As for me, I consider my book *On achève parfois ses romans en Italie* to be, through its form and content, a poetic tale. It is subdivided into five parts but, above all, it is composed of one hundred fragments.

In each one of these hundred fragments (the number of cantos in *The Divine Comedy*) the density and formal autonomy of the poem can be found. Each fragment – referring to Sienna, San Gimignano, Venice, Trieste or Milan – can be read independently of the story, like a poem in a poetry book. That's why I talk about it being a poetic novel. I worked very hard on the language. I particularly focused on the choice of words and rhythms. I'm looking to provide sensations and privileged moments rather than facts or intrigues. It's a necessary stage in my life. This novel is intimately linked to what has happened in my life and the changes I've lived through.

ANTONIO D'ALFONSO: To finish I'd like you to speak to me about the selection of texts translated by Christine Tipper that is soon to be published. What does it feel like to be in an "English" body, since language doesn't seem to me to be important for your identity? Do you recognize yourself in another language?

FRANCIS CATALANO: The book is called *Where Spaces Glow*. It's a *Selected Poems*. When I read my poems in English for the first time I felt doubly strange. In fact, I felt like a stranger in my own land. *(Laughter.)* I like this impression of disorientation that one finds when reading a translation of ones texts. Christine Tipper, who I was fortunate to meet in Barcelona and with whom I worked with on the texts, has translated my texts with sensitivity and intelligence.

English is a language that possesses great power through expression and suggestion. Under its apparent aridity flow unsuspected rivers. I am impressed by how that language manages, in a few words, to say the same things, to recreate the same shocks, but with this power of expression. I love this same quality of language when I read Shakespeare's Sonnets or, for example, Sylvia Plath.

Also it is very interesting that all translation questions identity. The writer, and certainly in a more immediate way, the translator is wrestling with a foreign language – that which she is translating. It is a language that must become hers, on which she will affix her name. Someone has already written: "The translator is the poet of poets." I believe it was Novalis. I don't know the context but I think that it means: only poets can understand the work involved. In a sense, in English, I feel both in a distant land and at home because these translations in this book published by Guernica connect with the poetic language that I imagined at the time I wrote those poems.

Translated from the French by Christine Tipper

This interview was first published in a slightly different form and in French in *Panoram Italia Montreal,* Vol. 8 No. 2 (April-May 2013), commissioned by editor Gabriel Riel-Salvatore, whom we thank for granting us the permission to reprint it here.

ABOUT THE AUTHOR

Montreal-born poet and translator Francis Catalano is the author of five poetry collections. His poems are regularly published in anthologies in Canada and elsewhere (South America, Europe). His translation of the *Didascalie per la lettura di un giornale / Instructions for Reading a Newspaper* by Italian poet Valerio Magrelli in 2006 earned him the John Glassco translation prize, awarded by the Literary Translators' Association of Canada. In 2010 he was awarded the Grand Prix Quebecor at the 26th International Festival of Poetry of Trois-Rivières for *qu'une lueur des lieux,* which was also short-listed for the Governor-General's Award. He is a member of the editorial committee of the poetry review *Exit.* Recently Francis published his first prose work, *On achève parfois ses romans en Italie.* Poems taken from *Romamor* (1999), *Index* (2001) and *qu'une lueur des lieux* (2010) are included in this collection.

ABOUT THE TRANSLATOR

A member of the Society of Authors, Christine Tipper is an accomplished translator, translating French-Canadian and Belgian writers. She has translated several authors for Guernica, including Nadine Ltaif *(Changing Shores)*, Evelyne Wilwerth *(Smile, You're Getting Old)*, and Danielle Fournier *(We Come From The Same Light)*. She has also had her own poems published in several collections and anthologies.

Printed in June 2013
by Gauvin Press,
Gatineau, Québec